The Branding of Polaroid

How we beat Eastman Kodak and its little yellow boxes in the marketplace despite a clunky product and an irrelevant corporate name.

by Paul Giambarba

Library of Congress Control Number 2014912422
ISBN No. 978-0-87155-001-9

Much of the following material first appeared on the Internet at:
http://giam.typepad.com/the_branding_of_polaroid_/
and in The Branding of Polaroid 1957—1977
privately printed by the author.

Author as metaphor
Third and revised edition, September 2014

Apologia

This little book is meant to be a personal look at an unusual client-designer relationship that endured from 1955 to 1983, in which there were 20 years that I can refer to as *The Branding of Polaroid 1957-1977*.

The best product photos were taken by Mel Goldman, a friend and former studio mate, who supplied Polaroid Corporation with much of its photography in the two decades of work shown in this book. I plead guilty for all the rest.

I must add that *Polaroid* is a registered trademark of Polaroid Corporation; *Cromalin* is a registered trademark of DuPont; *Color-Key* is a registered trademark of 3-M; *Impossible* is a trademark of The Impossible Project Gmbh; and let us not forget giant Eastman Kodak and their registered trademarks: *Kodachrome, Kodacolor,* and the rest.

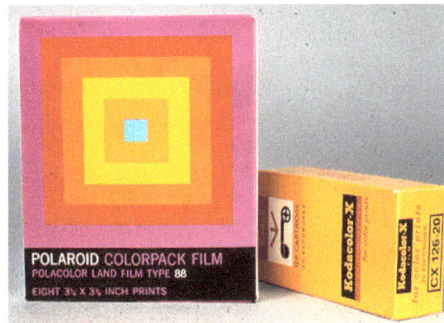

That which follows is a true story of how we beat their little yellow boxes at point of purchase.

Contents

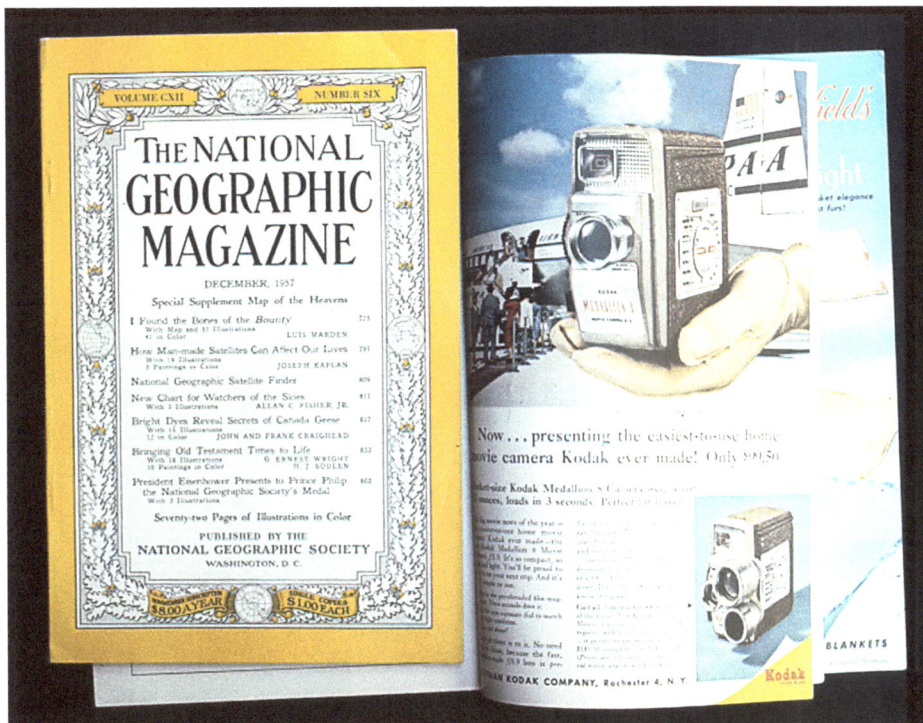

Imagery: Polaroid's Lack of Brand

It's important to remember what advertising looked like in 1957. Kodak's product design bore traces of industrial styling that was called streamlining. Pan American Airlines was still calling itself PAA and the National Geographic Magazine's cover design was in a static format that hadn't changed in decades.

In 1957, and for prior decades, the photographic marketplace was saturated in Eastman Kodak yellow. Polaroid's pre-1958 packaging featured red and gray (the school colors of the Massachusetts Institute of Technology) and little crossed circular filters—a hold-over from Polaroid's polarization products—along with the imponderable name in an illegible typeface. As might be expected, Kodak yellow sat like an elephant on the few Polaroid packages at point of purchase.

Stores where photo products were sold were saturated in Kodak yellow.

There are two designers who are considered geniuses: one is the person who conceived of Eastman's yellow boxes, and the other* was responsible for Howard Johnson's orange roof. Could anyone come up with anything better?

---

* I'm guessing, but I think it was Frank Gianinnoto.

Americans eventually learned how to pronounce this tricky name, although it may have taken a decade to do so. Like nuclear, a word that some of our presidents have never learned to correctly pronounce, Polaroid often came out poyle-a-rode. The company had its origins in the polarization process for which Edwin Land and his associates produced material used in World War II. There's much more to it than that, but that's the short answer. It's the brand name we were forced to work with. If you think this is bad, wait until you see the packaging on the pages that follow. That logo (see page 9) in use until 1958, had been set in a typeface in which the lower case "a" is barely distinguishable from a lower case "o."

Seeing this ineffectual treatment for brand identification where a potential customer has only a fraction of a second to register an impression, favorable or otherwise, gave me the courage to tackle the problem. Hell, I thought, I certainly can't do any worse than that. Stan Calderwood later told me that the original concept wasn't even challenged when it was presented to Polaroid management. After all, aren't red and gray MIT's school colors?

9

POLAROID

My simple solution was to set it in the only decent sans serif face that was available to us at the time, *News Gothic*. Restrained and classy, *News Gothic* is also distinctly American, one of several faces designed by the great type designer, Morris Fuller Benton (1872 - 1948) and cut by American Type Founders Co. There were other versions of this face, the most common substitute at the time being *Trade Gothic,* Mergenthaler's linotype product identifed as "after M.F. Benton." I specified the authentic ATF version from Boston's best typesetter, H.G. McMennamin.

These film boxes illustrate how vulnerable Polaroid products were at point of purchase in a marketplace dominated by Eastman Kodak's yellow boxes.

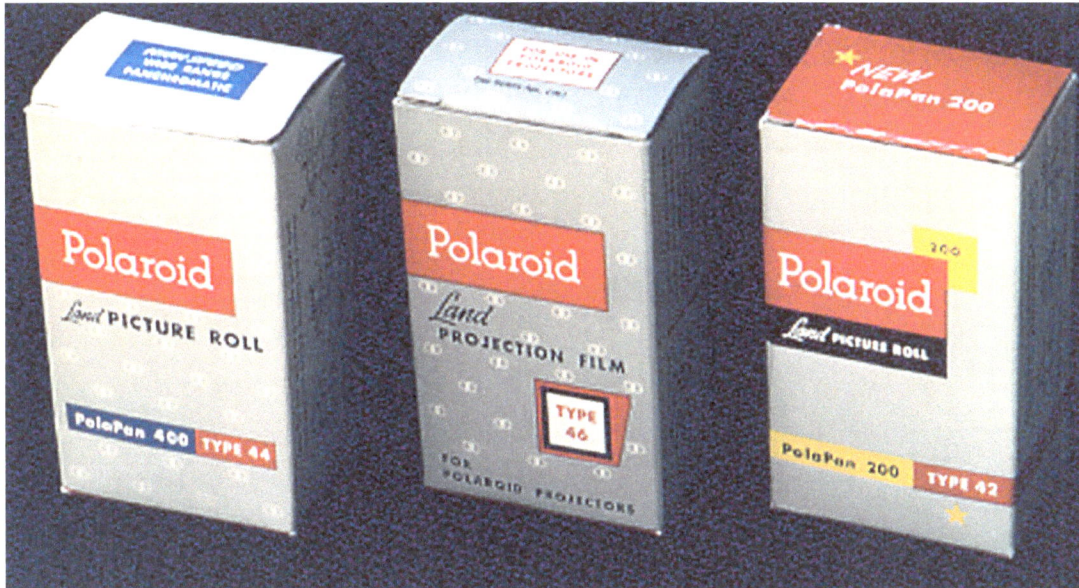

There was no consistency in how they used the soap bubbles (see page 9) on a gray background. Some grays were darker than others and then the bubbles disappeared altogether. Polaroid in Memphis was still a typographic disaster. Note NEW on top of the right-hand box. The sales department really never ever outgrew that.

Branding Polaroid Without a Thought Given to Clarity and Comprehension

Polaroid package design looked like this when I got the go-ahead to redesign the line. White crossed filters denoting polarizing filters looked like soap bubbles against a drab gray background. Polaroid is dropped-out, or reversed, from a red patch in a mindlessly vandalized version of a typeface called *Memphis*. The true *Memphis* lower case "a" has an upper serif to distinguish it from an "o," but close inspection will reveal that the upper serif has been removed from the Polaroid "a." Thus the brand name could be easily misread at quick glance as Poloroid. Of all the counterproductive things one can do in commerce, this was outrageously mindless, especially when considering the cost to launch a new line of products.

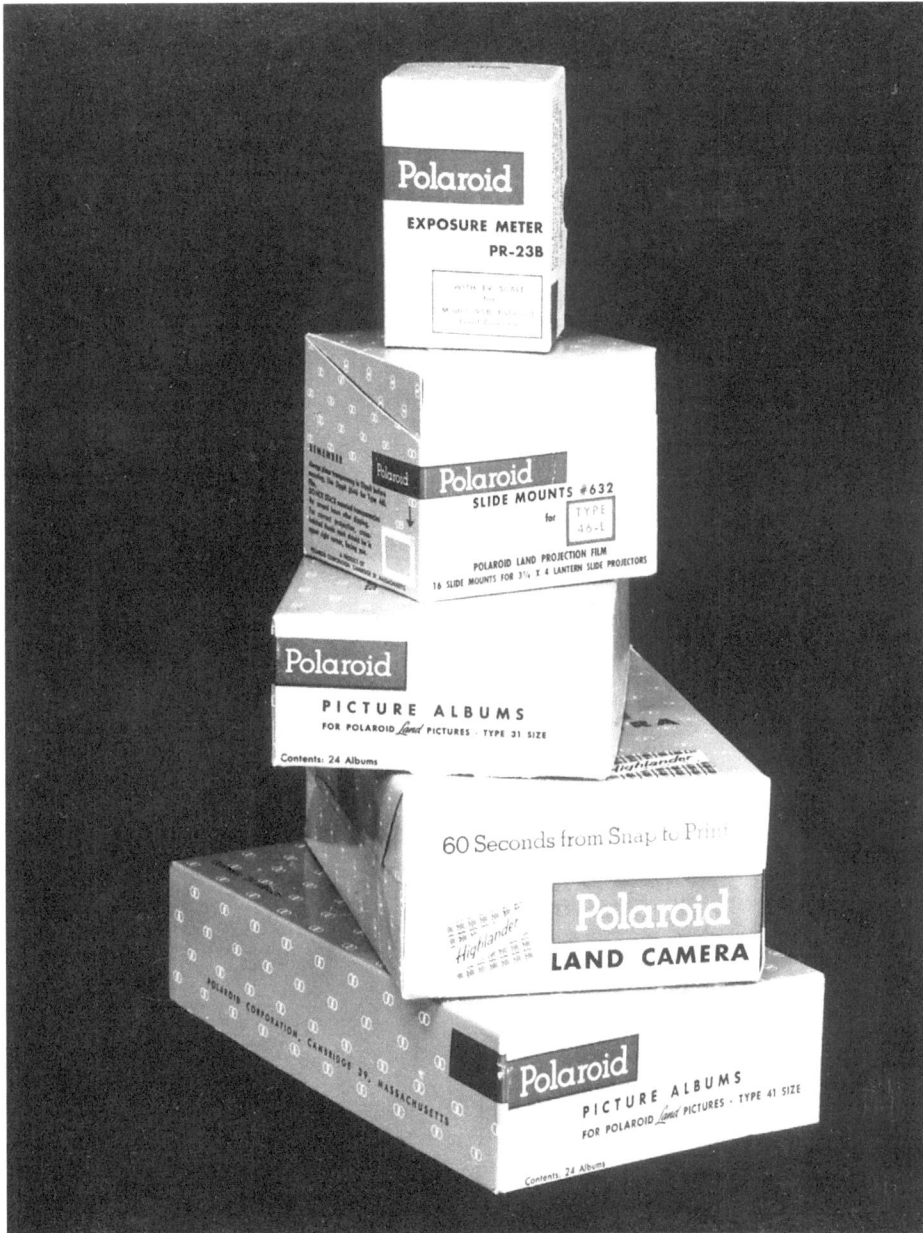

POLAROID was purposely set in caps to give a consumer some help in identifying and perhaps even remembering the brand name.

I took a lot of flak in meetings from resident MBAs who had read Motivational Research Institute founder, Freudian disciple and business guru Ernst Dichter (1907-1991), who had proclaimed from on high that black was a morbid color and should not be used in the marketplace. (Dichter worked with Ford on the Edsel.)

It took only about ten years for black packaging to become extremely popular for photo products as designer and art directors became aware of the possibilites of black as a display color to combat Eastman Kodak yellow.

Imitation is the sincerest form of flattery.

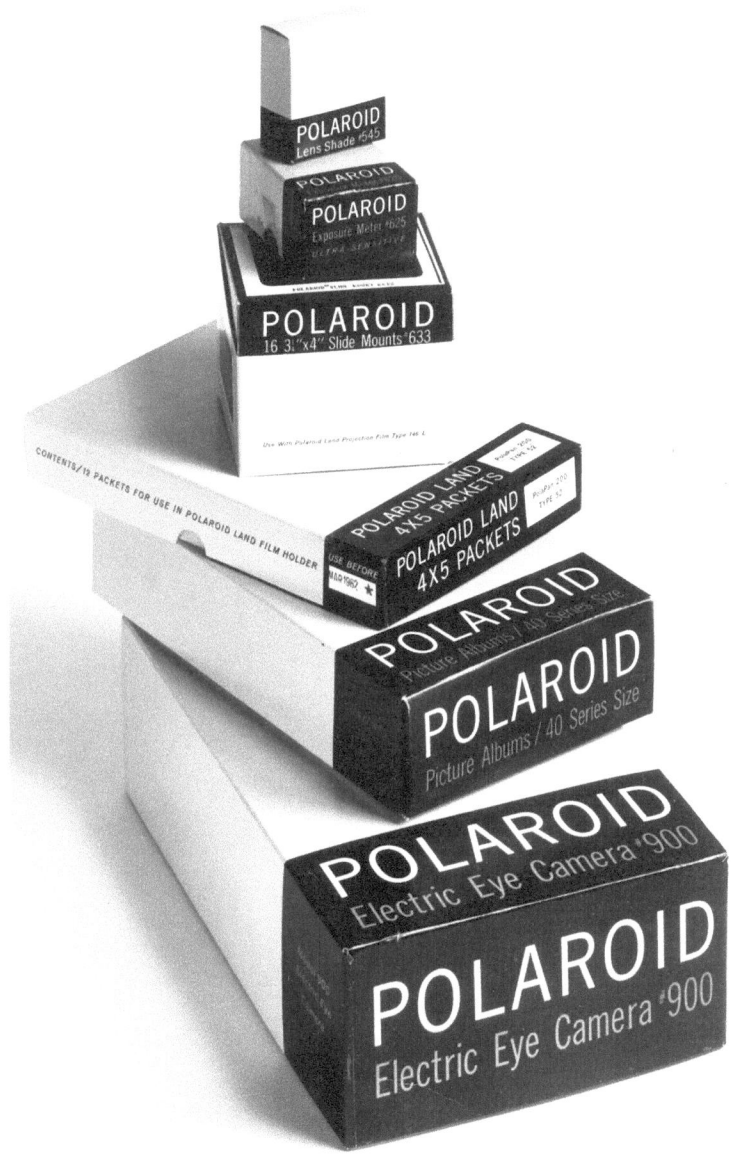

POLAROID
Lens Shade #545

POLAROID

POLAROID
Exposure Meter #625
ULTRA SENSITIVE

POLAROID
16 3¼"x4" Slide Mounts #633

Use With Polaroid Land Projection Film Type 146 L

CONTENTS/10 PACKETS FOR USE IN POLAROID LAND FILM HOLDER

POLAROID LAND
4X5 PACKETS

POLAROID LAND
4X5 PACKETS

USE BEFORE
MAY 1962 ★

POLAROID
Picture Albums / 40 Series Size

POLAROID
Picture Albums / 40 Series Size

POLAROID
Electric Eye Camera #900

POLAROID
Electric Eye Camera #900

Fortunately, Stan Calderwood overruled the Dichter *Amen Chorus*. He could see the importance of fighting back against Eastman and how well the end panels would show up on television, where he had planned to spend some money.

It must be remembered that television images were only black-and-white at the time.

Perry Como, left, and Steve Allen were Polaroid TV spokespersons.

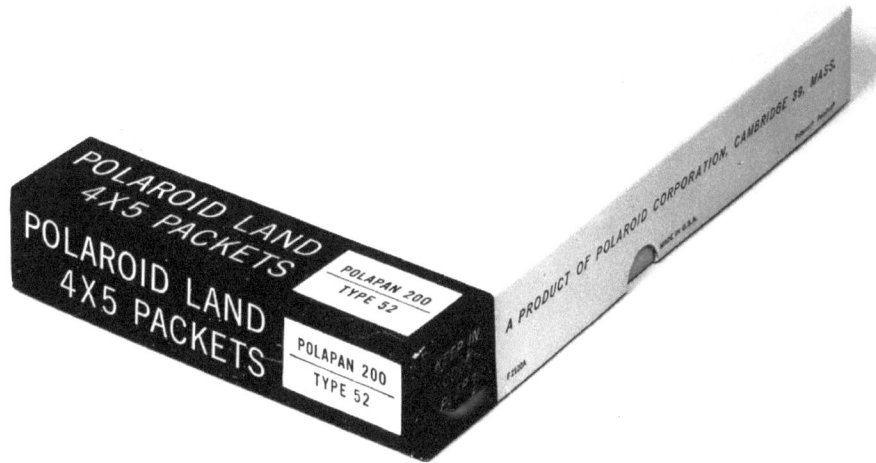

This is the first film box that I did in the format that featured the new black end panels. Virtually all professional photographers depended upon 4 x5 film to test their lighting before loading their Calumet, Linhof *or* Sinar *view cameras with conventional wet-chemistry film.*

Professional photographers working for Polaroid, such as Ansel Adams and Marie Cosindas, also used this film for final prints.

The Package Design Prototype that I Developed in 1958 for all Camera Models and Accessories

The first hardware package that I designed in 1958.

The product sits on top of the package which also functions as a case or counter display that identifies it and its use when exhibited in a camera store.

POLAROID
Land Camera Model 110A

POLAROID
Land Camera Model 110A

Pathfinder

This was my solution for getting Polaroid into some decent packaging with a chance of developing product identity and the branding we hear so much about today.

Gray was retained only for continuity, the black end panels to subdue Kodak yellow that saturated every marketplace and upstaged the drab over-all gray and soap bubbles of earlier Polaroid packaging.

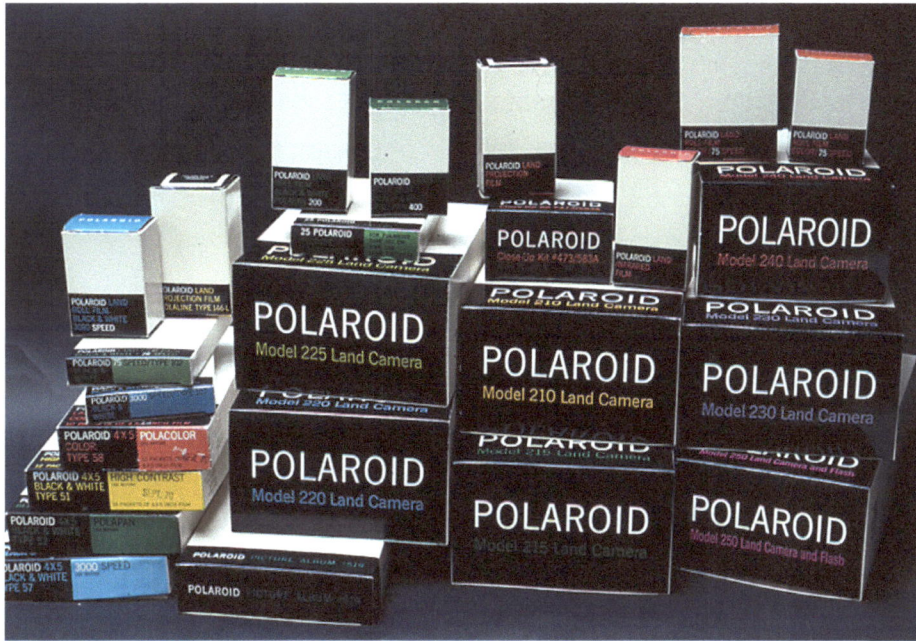

The 200 line of Polaroid Land Cameras came soon on the heels of the family of 100s. I remember asking at the time why there were so many models of virtually the same camera. Price points was the answer, and besides, the shop cost to attach new face plates was relatively little compared to the sales incentives provided by being able to say "New." At the time, most Polaroid cameras were manufactured by U.S. Time, makers of Timex watches..

To Logo or Not to Logo

Stan Calderwood and I spent a lot of time considering the pros and cons of logos. We came to the conclusion that Polaroid would be better off if we didn't paint ourselves into a corner with a logo that might be appropriate for a few years, then less so as time went on.

The first order of business was to create a brand name image that people could remember and correctly pronounce: Pola-royd, not Poy-la-rode. Next, we should have signage at every retail outlet that was clean and classy.

This was easier said than done. Almost every supplier of extruded plastic and aluminum signage wanted to sell us a version of their all-purpose tavern sign with phony waterfalls and stary skies. After considerable struggle we prevailed, and these signs appeared at most stores.

POLAROID
LAND CAMERAS

POLAROID
LAND
CAMERAS

POLAROID
LAND
CAMERAS

YOUR
STORE
NAME

Will Burtin (1902-1972), a great designer and early art director of *Fortune* magazine said, it would not have been possible to create monumental work as he did for Container Corporation of America without the total support and cooperation of Walter Paepcke (1896-1960), president of CCA.

Stan Calderwood made my work a breeze. He was the in-house power that caused all the good things that happened for Polaroid Corporation in its golden years.

549 Tech Square, Cambridge. When Polaroid finally moved into some new digs, the Sales and Advertising departments were housed in the overhang directly ahead. There used to be meter parking readily available at first, but as more troops moved in, a large parking lot was opened up behind the building. The wind was fierce because it blew down a tunnel created by the many buildings. Carrying a full sheet of illustration board was akin to being on a wind-surfer.

The Players: Call Me Doctor

Edwin Herbert Land *was* Polaroid. The corporation was his sand box—he could do just as he pleased, which is how the cost of producing SX-70 and Polavision got the company into financial trouble decades later.

But this was 1957.

Polaroid Corporation reported gross sales of $48,043,000 —up from $34,000,000 the year before, and almost twice that of 1955 at $26,421,000—when I first met Stan Calderwood and began freelancing the account. Edwin H. Land was called Dr. Land by all who worked at Polaroid, but he had not earned a doctorate of any kind at this time, though later he was the recipient of significant honorary degrees.

Edwin Land was a very photogenic CEO.
His demeanor was authoritarian—corporate officers were expected
to jump at his commands, day and night, 24/7.

This portrait is a portion of a photo copyright McGraw-Hill for
Business Week's 15 April 1972 issue, the photographer unidentified.

This is not to diminish his importance as one of the country's great scientists and inventors, but it seemed a bit much on this side of the Atlantic. I'm not aware that he was ever heard to say, "For goodness sake, stop calling me Doctor."

There is much biographical material on Edwin Herbert Land on *Google*, *Yahoo* and other search engines for those who wish to read more about his accomplishments.

I would also recommend the excellent book about Land by Peter C. Wensberg: *Land's Polaroid*, Houghton Mifflin, 1987; and the more detailed title by Victor K. McElheny: *Insisting on the Impossible*, Perseus Publishing, 1998. I'm quite certain that this phrase of Land's has had much to do with Dr. Florian Kaps' naming his endeavor into instant analog photography, *The Impossible Project*. (See page 133.)

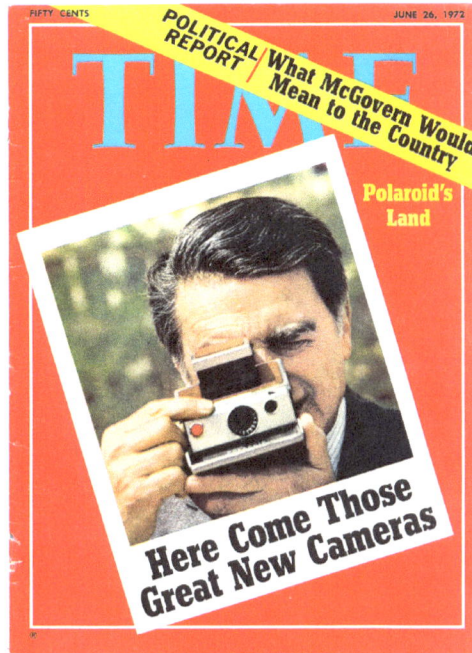

Time *Magazine of June 26, 1972 devoted a cover and pages 80 through 88 in its Business section to a Marketing/Cover story:* Polaroid's Big Gamble on Small Cameras. *This doesn't make a whole lot of sense—it was bigger than many popular models of snapshot cameras and as heavy as most. OK, it folded up, but so did the other Polaroid models. If it did fit into a pocket, as claimed, it needed a big pocket that was securely attached to the jacket.*

I met Edwin Land on a couple of rare occasions. Once I sat in on a meeting with him and the art director of *Scientific American*.

They were certain that the colors one would see on the moon would differ from the colors we perceive here on earth. I've often wondered how they reconciled the photos from the moon that we all saw on television a decade later.

To be honest, I must admit that at the time I had no idea what they were talking about.

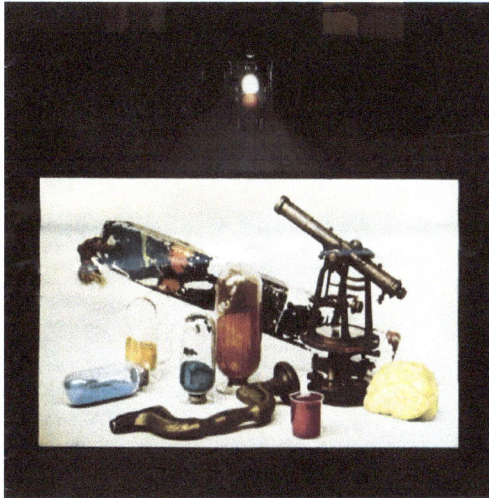

SCIENTIFIC AMERICAN

FULL COLOR FROM RED AND WHITE · FIFTY CENTS · *May 1959*

The cover of Scientific American *for May 1959. Inside is a 14-page article,* Experiments in Color Vision *by Edwin H. Land. (No doctor titles for this audience.) I once sat through a slide show he put on for us demonstrating how he achieved full color when only red and white images were projected on a screen and appeared in full color.*

On a social occasion, we met again while attending the wedding of a Polaroid product manager. As Land was taking photos with a previously under-wraps SX-70 camera, a cheeky female guest (my late wife, Ruth) was heard to ask, "Do you suppose it will work?"

Nobody laughed.

Edwin H. Land did not appear to be overly amused.

I thought to myself, "There goes that account!"

I waited for the other shoe to drop but it did not. Apparently, Land didn't take names. Bless him for that. (I later learned that "Do you suppose it will work?" was an inside joke among some of the product engineers.)

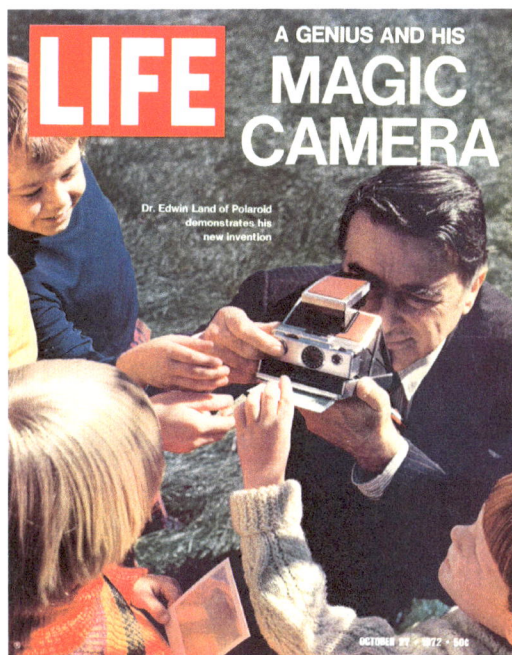

Life *Magazine for October 27, 1972. The sub-head reads:* Dr. Edwin Land of Polaroid demonstrates his new invention. *(It was to a posed group of children clutching at an emerging print.) Pages 42 through 48 include a portfolio of photos, an opening spread with a headline in huge type, all caps: DR. LAND'S LATEST BIT OF MAGIC, and a full page of his words of wisdom under the heading, "If you are able to state a problem, it can be solved.*

Land's Management Style

The good doctor was famous for pitting his executives against one another. In the course of my years freelancing other accounts, I often had the misfortune of being forced to listen to lesser executives extolling this as a courageous business command-and-control procedure. I thought it nonsensical and sadistic.

Polaroid Corporation execs didn't exactly set the world on fire once they left the nest. Someimes they found slots in lofty top management of *Fortune 100* companies, but I remember Stan Calderwood being very vocal—perhaps as sour grapes—
"I should have fired that clown when he worked for me."

Land also put his lab rats through the wringer when he insisted they could paint full color pictures with only a tube each of red and white paint because he used only red and white filters to create full-color images by projection (see page 31).

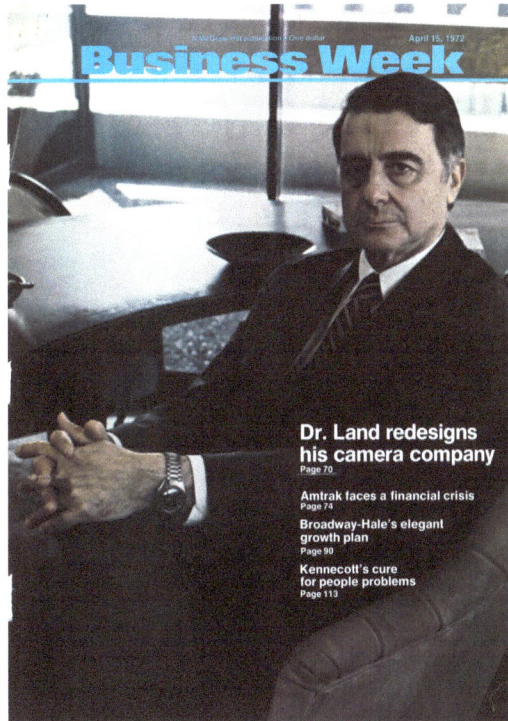

© McGraw-Hill

Business Week *for April 15, 1972 gave Land pages 70 through 73
with the sub-head:* Polaroid puts $200 million into producing its
new camera. . . . *Under a photo of Land the caption reads,
"Polaroid's Dr. Land: 'There will be as many Alladins [code name for
SX-70] sold as there are telephones.'"*

Bob Casselman

The late Robert C. Casselman (dates unknown) was Polaroid's Vice President of Sales in 1957. (Stan Calderwood reported to him.) Bob had movie star good looks and a pleasant demeanor, and although he could be very difficult, I didn't have any trouble from him because I don't think he knew exactly what I was up to. Stan was great at office politics and probably assured him that I was a very affordable expense. Bob came to Polaroid from Lever Brothers, manufacturers of soap products, the most famous of which was *Lifebuoy*, heavily advertised on radio where it claimed that its use prevented body odor. A fog horn ominously bleated *beeee-oooo* behind the voice-over of the announcer. Lever was comfortable with that kind of advertising. Their entire Cambridge operation moved out one day, stranding many experienced employees who were forced to find employment elsewhere. In Bob Casselman's case it was in the same Cambridge neighborhood. It was obvious to all that Stan Calderwood chafed at his role as underling and wanted Bob's job. It didn't take long for that to happen.

This photo of Bob Casselman was taken on Polaroid roll film Type 42 in 1958.

Stan Calderwood

Stanford Matson Calderwood was the in-house power who made all things possible and the driving force in creating brand for Polaroid. More pertinent and personal information follows in the next few pages.

Stan at his desk in the former warehouse building at 119 Windsor
 Street.I took this with my old Hasselblad Superwide, vintage 1950;
the best camera I ever owned. It gets in all the detail that make
wide-angle lenses so practical. On the desk is his favorite pencil,
a big black Eberhard Faber Ebony (no. 6325) that he used for his
notes and copy mark-ups. His bold messages never left any doubt
about what he wanted and when he wanted it.

Stan Calderwood used photography in diverse and humorous ways. This is his most frequently used postcard. The message was written by Peg Baker, his secretary of many years. It reads:

"Dear Giam —
Stan is so despondent without you.
Peg"

[Interesting to note that he hadn't quite got to know how my name was spelled. I was in San Francisco checking up on camera stores to determine what we needed for point-of-purchase displays.]

A Polaroid photo or copy could be attached to the back of the pressure-sensitive adhesive back of a Polacard, *shown on page 40.*

Stan was the best client I ever had and it resulted in the best work I have ever done. Stan had been a communications officer on the heavy cruiser, U.S.S. *Minneapolis*, during World War II. He had been through harrowing action in the Pacific, particularly when the ship was relentlessy attacked by *kamikaze* pilots off Leyte in the Philippine Islands. When the war was over and the "Minnie" docked in a Chinese port, he cut orders for himself that allowed him to travel in northern China. He was very proud of this escapade and, with Norma Jean, sent amusing postcards from all over the world. He then had a rubber stamp made that read: "This sure is a nifty place." See bottom of next page.

Earlier, after receiving his commission as an ensign, he reported for training at Harvard College where a radio school was conducted by Dave Garroway, who later became the first host of NBC's *Today* show. In the early 1950s, Stan achieved fame in New England as a reporter when he scooped all the competing papers with a confession by Dr. Herman Sanders, who had hastened the death of a terminally ill patient. This was the first case of euthanasia to make national headlines. Stan worked for the irascible William Loeb at the *Manchester Union-Leader*, then *United Press*, freelancing magazines when he could. Stan arrived at Polaroid after doing public relations at *Eastern Gas and Fuel Associates*.

Calderwood as world traveler. The Polaroid photo is not well coated.

Bill Field

Bill said he wanted to be a graphic designer when I first met him, and asked if he could work for me in the art department. Bill was a Harvard graduate who majored in anthropology after a hitch in the army during the Korean War. He was extremely agreeable as well as industrious, and he also possessed the intellectual curiosity a designer needs to be successful.

When I left to work at my studio on Cape Cod, Bill took over as art director, later design director, and had a fabulous career.

I could not have done all that I did without him.

Bill on the phone at 549 Tech Square, Cambridge, 1972.

Bill Field eventually left Polaroid to return to his native Santa Fé, New Mexico to start his own shop. He also became director of the *Museum of Spanish Colonial Art*, the first museum of its kind to celebrate the rich cultural life of Spanish New Mexico.

Peter Wensberg

Peter showed up a bit later in 1958 when I recruited him for Stan.

He was assistant sales promotion manager at the Boston publishing house of *Little, Brown and Company* at the time and we had become friends after I had done freelance artwork for him. He was great to work for, and there are never enough clients like that. Besides being one of the best and the brightest, he was always fair and accommodating.

Peter Wensberg spent 24 years at Polaroid directing marketing and communications. He left in 1982 as Executive Vice President two months after Edwin Land retired. He then joined *Warner Communications* as president of *Atari Tel*, a division of *Atari*.

He was the author of *Land's Polaroid*, and a novel, *The Last Bastion*.

Peter died 8 November 2006 at the age of 77.

Rest in peace, good friend.

Peter Wensberg at Polaroid, 1972.

Paul Giambarba

"Please, Nikolai. It can never be."

NOVEMBER 19, 1956   31

Full page cartoon in Sports Illustrated *for the 19 November 1956 Melbourne Olympics issue. Caption: "Please, Nikolai. It can never be."*

Before I got involved with Polaroid, I had a successful career freelancing Boston advertising agencies and publishers, as well as national magazines such as *Sports Illustrated, True,* and *This Week,* a Sunday newspaper supplement, with the largest circulation of any publication at the time. Calderwood had also freelanced, as a photojournalist, so we had this much in common. He was also impressed with the work and study I had done in Europe on my own, and my pragmatic design philosophy—*Less is More.*

At work in my Everett Street, Cambridge, studio-workshop, 1960.

"Well," you might say, " It takes a lot of hubris to include yourself among those corporate types." I agree, but I would like to make the point that I began with nothing more than blank paper and some typewritten words supplied me.

Within a year after I created a functioning art department and the start of a production department, two more rookies were added to the roster. Bill Field and Peter Wensberg. Actually, Bill had already been working as a copywriter for Jim Rosenfield, Stan Calderwood's assistant ad guy, whom he recruited from *CBS*. I recruited Peter from the Boston publisher, *Little, Brown*.

With Stan Calderwood managing the team, it soon became as good a company as a clueless 1958 Polaroid Corporation had any right to expect.

Trade and Dealer Advertising

We have the new Polaroid Color Pack Camera: the most advanced camera in the world!

Color pictures in 50 seconds, black-and-white in 10, yet it weighs less than many 35mm cameras.

Come in and try it today at

Dealer Name

My dealer ad for Polaroid Land Camera Model 100—the best of all camera models, in my opinion. See pages 78 - 82 for more about this illustration technique.

Stan's first move to create a strong and contemporary image for Polaroid was to fire BBD&O, the Boston advertisng agency of record and hire Doyle, Dane and Bernbach (DD&B) after a careful survey of ad agencies throughout the country. This is the work of their principal art director, Bob Gage. It was a trade ad that appeared in photography magazines, what we called hobby books, and it proved to me that Stan had the necessary taste as well as ambition to create great advertising and sales promo.

This ad was a stunner for 1958.

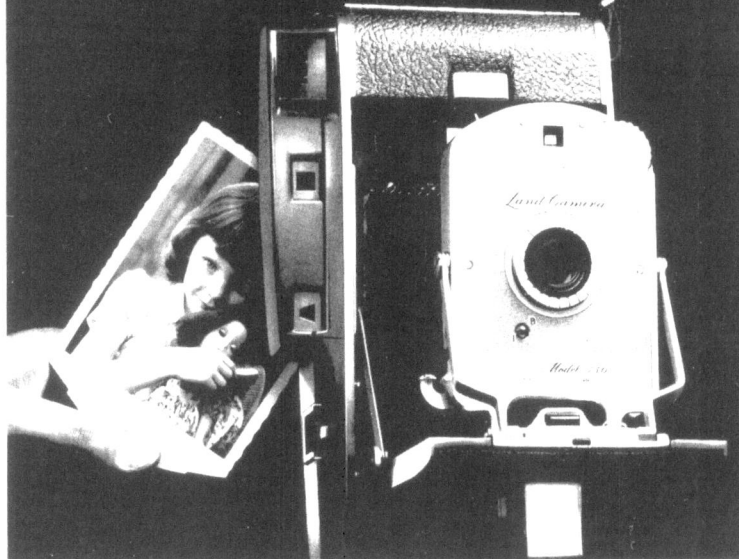

Announcing a new model Polaroid Land Camera

The 150

Hᴇʀᴇ is a particularly fine 60-second camera made especially for the discerning picture-taker. It has a coupled rangefinder—long-base, unit power, super-imposed-image type, operated by a smooth action focusing knob on the camera bed. The same motion also automatically aims the viewfinder to eliminate parallax and insure accurate composition. The camera has an excellent, coated triplet lens of high resolving power (modified Cooke design).

The new features of the model 150 Polaroid Land Camera assure you of sharp, excellently composed pictures. Loaded with the new high-speed panchromatic Polaroid Land film, this camera will produce pictures of a quality you'll find difficult to match.

Make it a point to visit your photo store and see this new model Polaroid Land Camera. Take a couple of shots with it yourself. We think you'll be quite impressed with how far 60-second photography has advanced . . . with how fine a precision instrument you can own for only $109.95.

Mucking Out the Polaroid Sales Promo Stable

This is the type of dealer ad that Polaroid sales managers of that period insisted upon. They claimed that dealers would only run crap, to use the operative term of those days. They were adamant that dealers would never run any kind of classy ad. I worked hard at convincing Stan Calderwood that this was nonsense. It was counterproductive to strive for a positive upmarket image and at the same time cave in to a messy, confusing and hysterical approach to sales promotion. The crappy ads had many vocal defenders, but Stan took them on and fought for our cause.

He won the war and Polaroid dealer ads were never the same.

These are some of my dealer ads. The ads ran in 1959 and 1960. I think they were the best looking ads we did. Bill Field and Peter Wensberg came back from New York with excellent photos by the very talented photographer Wingate Paine. The model is very appealing and believable, and their copy is perfect.

A technical note to typophiles: To my knowledge these are among the first use of *Helvetica* type in the USA. I discovered *Neue Haas Grotesk* when it made its debut in Switzerland and contacted the type foundry in Basel. They directed me to a typophile in Cleveland, Roy Rothstein of *Type and Art*, who was setting it in *Didot*, the European equivalent of picas. I think this helped to further enhance a contemporary, clean and classy look to dealer ads.

Helvetica type is much too ubiquitous today, but in those days it made a very impressive statement.

If You Can AIM This Camera You've Got it Made!

The New Polaroid J66

This is the new Polaroid J66 – the simplest Land Camera ever made—and it actually costs about the same as the first Land Camera model introduced more than 12 years ago!

It takes the same large pictures – but with what a difference. It's fully automatic. There are no settings you have to make. An electric eye chooses the exposure. You don't even have to focus. You don't need an expensive light meter. The flash gun is built in too. And your picture is ready in just 10 seconds.

There are 12 years of improvements, refinements and brand new ideas in this camera. And yet it actually costs about the same as the first Land Camera on the market.

If you've always wanted a Polaroid Land Camera—and who hasn't?—this is your chance. Come in for a free 10 second demonstration.

FULLY AUTOMATIC

COSTS ABOUT $90

SIMPLEST LAND CAMERA EVER

NO FOCUSING, NOTHING TO SET

10-SECOND PICTURES

Dealer Name

Stan came by my temporary office one day and asked if I could come up with an idea or two for magazine ads that show how polarizing works in sunglasses.

This is a page from *Elle*, the French magazine for women, that probably goes back to 1958 or 1959.

I think the ad was produced by DD&B because that is one good-looking young woman.

But I digress …

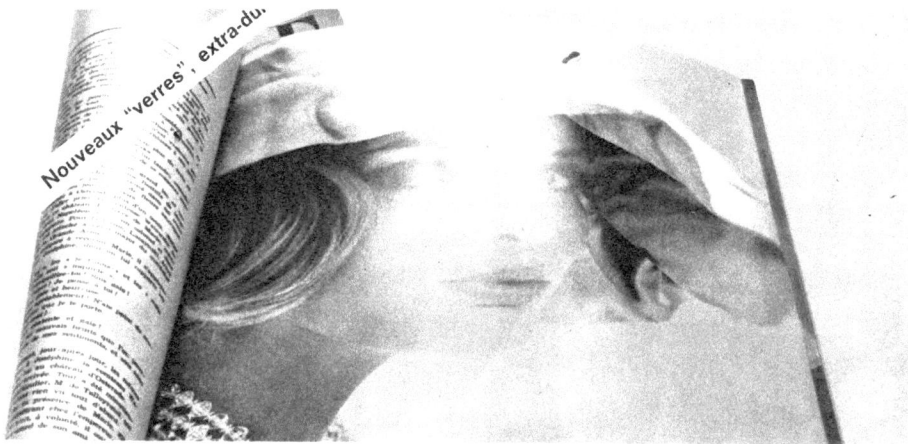

Si la réverbération vous éblouit...

...avec les lunettes de soleil Polaroid vous verrez clairement

"Polaroid" Marque Déposée

Faites cet essai avec un magazine sur papier glacé : sous certains angles les reflets de la lumière vous éblouissent, gênant la vision. Mettez des lunettes Polaroid : tout éblouissement disparaît.

C'est qu'elles sont faites sur un principe spécial : elles *sélectionnent* les rayons lumineux, au lieu de simplement les colorer. La lumière utile (celle qui vous permet de voir clairement) les traverse, mais les réverbérations horizontales sont absorbées par leur filtre optique spécial.

Avec des lunettes de soleil Polaroid vous voyez mieux, vous voyez des détails qui vous échappaient et vos yeux y gagnent en confort et sécurité car les lunettes Polaroid sont légères, optiquement correctes, sans distorsion, et incassables.

Partout où il y a réverbération, portez vos lunettes Polaroid (sur les lunettes correctrices montez seulement nos "clip-overs" Polaroid, tellement légers !).

Les nouvelles lunettes Polaroid super-résistantes sont en vente chez votre opticien-lunetier. **Lunettes de soleil Polaroid.**

155

59

Literature Pieces

There was also an immediate need to upgrade all the many lit pieces that were being generated by sales reps and middle managers in the ad and sales promotion departments.

Polaroid donated a lot of promotional material and production to serious publications devoted to fine photography.

This is an Arnold Newman photo of Pablo Picasso that was used by the Royal Photographic Society (UK) for the cover of one of its publications circa 1958.

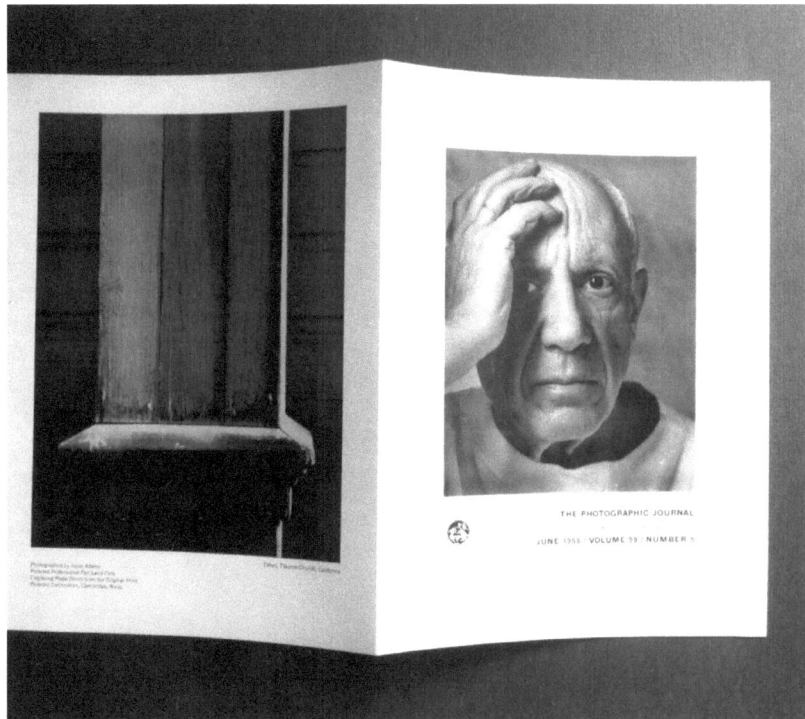

This publication did not have a newsstand sale. I placed the masthead, so to speak, below Picasso. The back cover is also a Polaroid photo, by Minor White. Most likely both photos were not taken with an off-the-shelf Polaroid Land Camera but were made with Polaroid Land 4x5 film utilizing a 4x5 back on a view camera.

The Polaroid MP-3 Multi-Purpose Industrial View Land Camera is overkill nomenclature for what was basically a Polaroid copy camera mounted on a sturdy metal and laminated wood base.

I had one for years—on loan—that I used to make 4x5 copy photos. Listed on the cover copy is a laundry list of all the things it will do.

The type is *Optima* and the photo is by Mel Goldman Studios, Boston.

MP-3

**Polaroid Multi-purpose
Industrial View Land Camera**

Ideal for:
slide-making
copying
small object photography
photomicrography
macrophotography
gross specimen photography
X-ray copying
wall chart copying
and many other uses

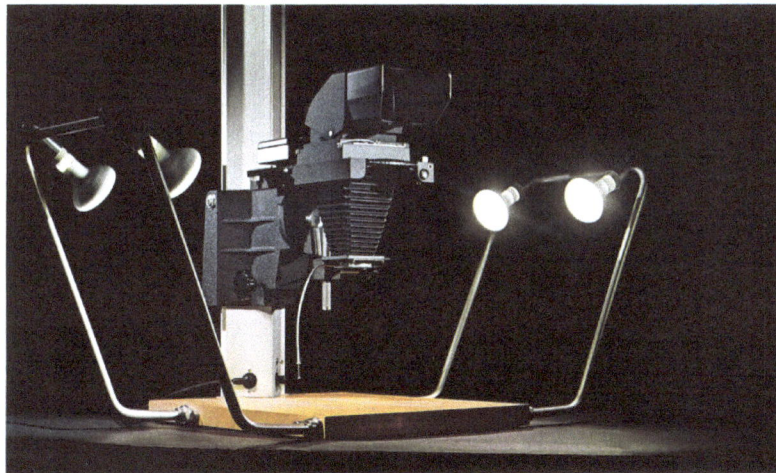

By the end of the 1960s, I was getting many lit pieces to do which required writing as well as design and production.

Since there was a demand for product and no one in-house with time to tackle such projects, they got farmed out to me.

One thing led to another and the next thing I knew I was assigned to produce, in its entirety, a 128-page *how-to* book.

Polaroid was supposed to supply the photos, as they had done for the two other pieces on the left, but in the end they came through with precious few. So guess who ended up trying to take usable Polaroid photos on Cape Cod where the skies are often burned out by haze?

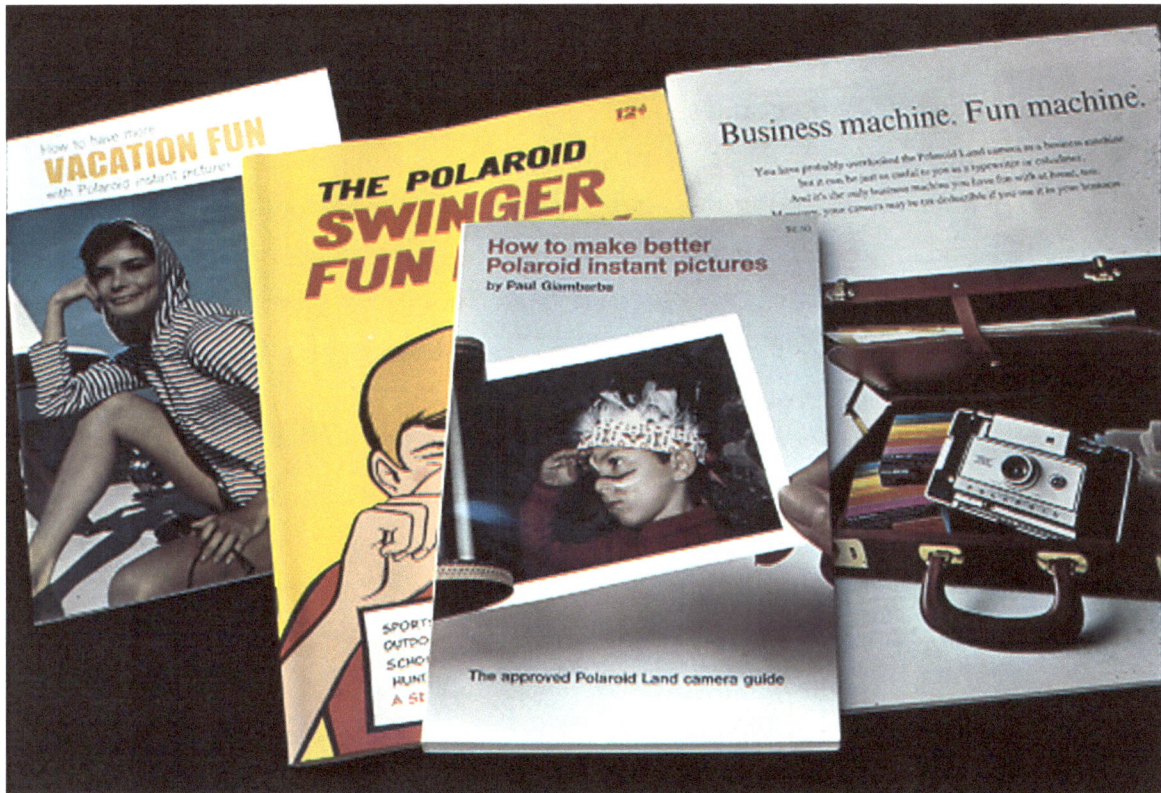

Literature pieces produced, 1969 and 1970. DD&B supplied the photo of the attaché case and the young woman. I used my own cartoons for the Swinger *comic book, and a photo of my son for the book on the right. More about that on the next page.*

One day at lunch, Peter Wensberg said that he would spend a million dollars to get customers to take cameras off the shelves in their hall closets and shoot a couple of rolls of film. I remembered those great Kodak books available at most camera stores and proposed doing a similar program for Polaroid. The concept was that they be sold as products, and the cost *self-liquidating*. Wensberg was elated at the results when I brought in the photos, dummy and script. Calderwood was equally enthusiastic.

At that point, Stan Calderwood had already decided to leave Polaroid. Had he stayed I'm sure he would have made it happen. Wensberg was busy preparing to take over Stan's job, and the entire book project died on the vine. I sold a trade edition to Doubleday anticipating promotional effort by Polaroid. It never materialized. Corporate envy might have been responsible for shooting down a project that control freaks couldn't smother the life out of.

(I did the book using only off-the-shelf Polaroid cameras. The cover photo is of my then five-year old son.)

$2.50

How to make better Polaroid instant pictures
by Paul Giambarba

The approved Polaroid Land camera guide

Where Were We Going?

By 1977, Stan Calderwood had been long gone, Bill Field was back home in Santa Fé, and I was dealing with yet another art director after his successor left. Products kept appearing out of left field such as this one, created to cozy up to independent camera stores, long ignored while Polaroid concentrated on major market distributors. I guess no one was paying a lot of attention so I was able to get away with naming store owners *CPS*s or *Certified Polaroid Specialists* on their phony diplomas.

By now Polaroid was falling upon hard times. Phone lines were eliminated, and for the first time I had to place calls to Accounts Payable to ask for payment of my past-due invoices.

The bean counters had taken over and it was evident that things would never be the same again.

What do we have here? First of all there's a slip case. In it are the following: a certificate for framing, a booklet of coupons, a window decal, a folder holding other decals such as hot numbers to attach to telephone dials, and various other folders promoting the Special Edition *program.*

Displays

Creating displays was also one of the ongoing assignments I got beginning in 1958, when I had the overall task of putting together an art department and a production department. (Until that time each middle manager took it upon himself to farm out art and design along with print production once the job was approved.)

The timer shown here first appeared in 1958. The card was laminated with a sheet of two-color printing—black and blue—with a die-cut for a plastic blister that held the product.

Copy appears to be hand-lettering plus *Alternate Gothic* in caps and *Franklin Gothic Italic*.

NEW POLAROID® TIMER

FITS ALL POLAROID LAND CAMERAS

Any timing up to two minutes
...ideal for either
regular or transparency films

Start and stop switch

$5⁹⁵

D238A

Printed in U.S.A.

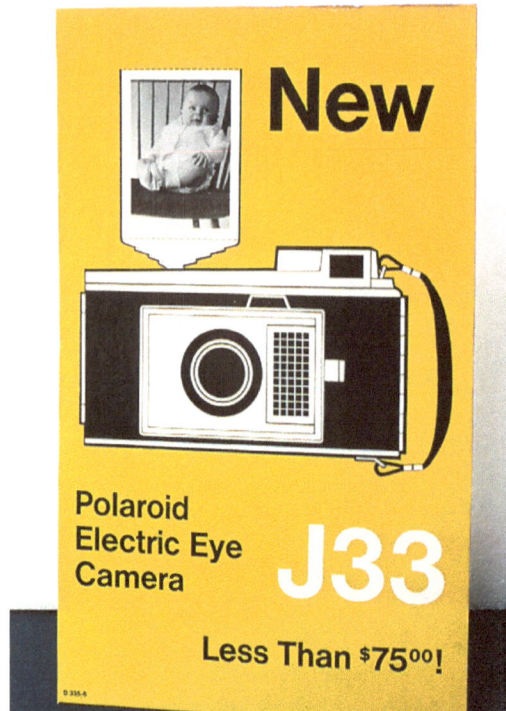

This counter card that promotes the first Polaroid cameras to utilize electric eye devices for better exposures. I did a version of my silhouette product illustrations and used a Polaroid photo of our infant daughter as well. The year is1961. The type is *Neue Haas Grotesk*, later known as *Helvetica*.

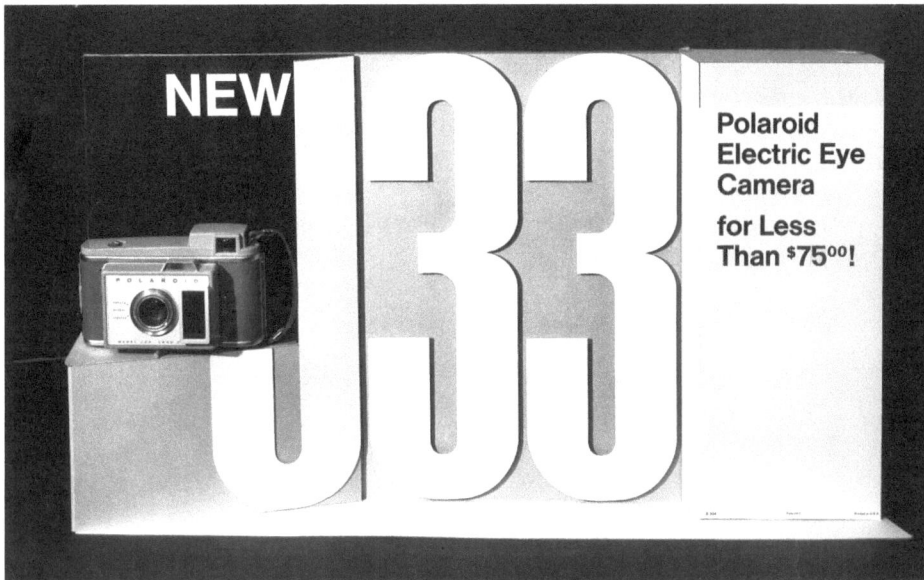

This is a much larger display that incorporates the use of an actual camera model.

The J33 is hand-lettered, something I don't think I do all that well. The type is also Neue Haas Grotesk, aka Helvetica.

1961 is the date. Two colors, yellow and black.

Designed for 1961, this still looks good today.

Another counter card in two colors, red and black.

You want simple?

This is simple.

Less *is* more.

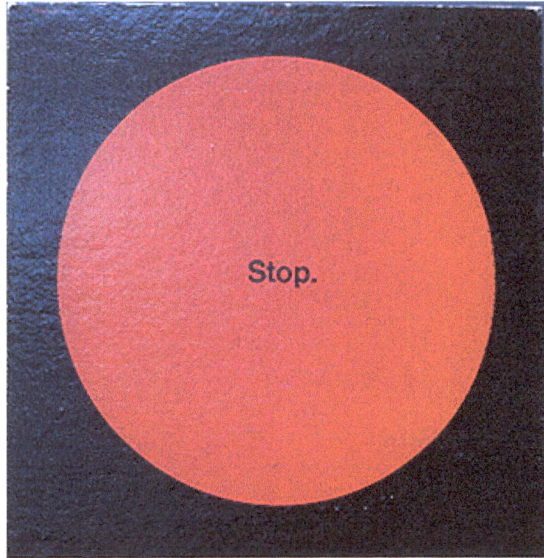

Stop.

Demonstration.
Polaroid Electric Eye
Land Camera.
This week only.
Your picture free.

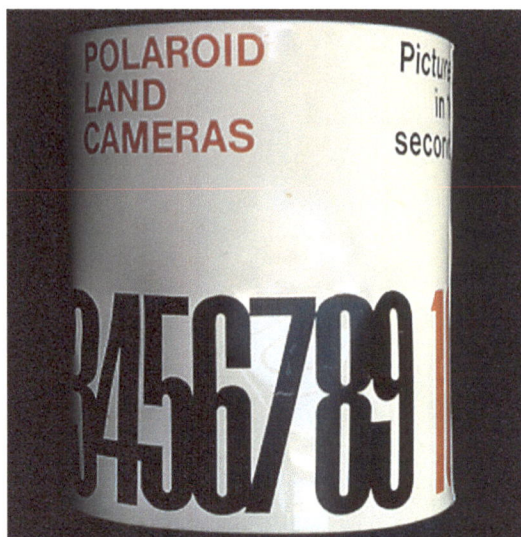

This revolving display also required my hand-lettering the numerals, another chore which took time and concentration. There was a small electric motor hidden inside the display which completed a revolution in exactly ten seconds. Prior to the introduction of this film, a full minute was required to fully process a Polaroid photo before it could be peeled apart from its paper negative.

Pictures
in 10
seconds

789 10 12

Problems with Letterpress and Newspaper Reproduction, and Silk Screen Printing

I think this came about after seeing and admiring so many ads in the *Neue Zürich Zeitung* daily newspaper (the Züri-Zeetig in Schweizerdeutsch) but that's a rough translation of a language I never could figure out because I lived for a time in Morges, near Lausanne, where French is the cantonal language.

This drawing was used for a silk-screened metal sign.

Polaroid Land Cameras

Polaroid Product Illustration

This is an example of an illustration technique I created to make a prosaic product look a lot stronger than it would in a traditional product photo. It's a pen-and-ink drawing made from measurements taken directly from the camera and stylized to create visual tension between the black solids and the white lines separating these solids. The Square Shooter had a one-piece plastic camera body that was used for all the Polaroid Colorpack line of cameras, with a different face plate added for each iteration. Square Shooter indicated that the camera used square format film that came along later when Polaroid wanted to lower its film prices (all based on the square inches or cm. of film used.) We also had the problem that I mentioned earlier of having to print by flexography on inexpensive board used for folding boxes.

Illustration for side panel of camera packaging, 1971.

This style of line illustration was effectively used in dealer ads where photo halftones printed poorly as letterpress in regional publications. The photo shows how impressive the line art was when enlarged for display purposes in trade shows.

Polaroid Product Identity

Integration of product lines of Polaroid Colorpack cameras made for the rectangular film size of 3-1/4 x 4-1/4 inches (cm. 8.6 x10.8) film size.

The Colorpack was the brain child of Stan Calderwood, then Executive Vice President of Polaroid Corporation. He shared this exalted role with William McCune, whose background was in engineering. McCune beat out Stan for the role of President when Edwin H. Land stepped down as CEO. I remember that there was a good deal of pressure for a film package with a four-color process photo on it. Peter Wensberg, his assistant Ted Voss, Design Director Bill Field and I discussed it and I was relieved to find that both Bill and I were of a mind to avoid the pretty picture. When I had something I thought still looked good the next morning, I brought it up to Cambridge for an evaluation. With Bill that took all of a couple of minutes—he was a quick study and decisive. Eventually we settled on six color stripes for Polacolor film and Colorpack camera boxes, and seven gradations of black ink for black-and-white film. These packages are shown on the preceding page and those that follow.

Colorpack II product image created in 1968. Illustration of camera model appears on side panel. A color photo could not be used due to the poor quality of the cardboard folding box.

Folding cameras, such as this Model 440, were at the high end of the the 400-series product price line. The sleeve held both camera and the Model 429 flash attachment.

In my opinion, these cameras—all clones of the original Model 100—took the very best Polaroid instant color photos, and all the hooplah about SX-70s and their spinoffs was more hubris than fact.

They were easier to use, too.

User-friendly— as we're prone to say today.

The Model 440 Polaroid Color Pack camera *was packaged in a sleeve with a flash attachment. There was a distinction between the folding* Color Pack *cameras and the one-piece plastic* Color-pack *cameras. As can be imagined, it led to a bit of confusion in the marketplace.*

It's not possible to describe a step-by-step scenario that led to the final design. Bill and I just kept trying to find something that would please us enough for him to bring into a meeting with Wensberg and Calderwood.

I had already been thinking of color and design as a corporate and/or product flag, as I did for Polaroid Sunglasses in 1962 (see page 127) for instant recognition by consumers at point-of-purchase where they might have only a fraction of a second to fall in love at first sight—in a manner of speaking. I began with blank folding box dummies supplied by Champion Paper Box, Polaroid's longtime supplier.

This is a dummy of a later Polaroid Pronto! Plus *camera display. It held a pack of* SX-70 *film and a camera. It rests on my drawing table on top of mechanicals made from my type proofs, then processed as* Cromalins. *Polaroid used these for product photography rather than wait for a box maker to supply press proofs.*

By 1970, the color stripes were a big hit. They were introduced into supermarkets, then big discount outlets and camera stores. Sales went through the roof until a recession set in and someone on high thought that Polaroid would sell even more film if it didn't cost so much since the money was in selling film and every square centimeter determines its cost to the consumer. Hence, square-format Polaroid film was born.

Bill Field gave me a blank box dummy in the new square format and said, "Maybe we ought to square-off the color stripes.

"See what you can do."

Square Shooter film packages for color and black and white flank camera boxes, 1970. I don't think it gets any better than this—I was worried about how I was going to cannibalize the color stripes without making a mess of things. You just don't know until you work at it and let it take you somewhere you hadn't contemplated. Design will often take on a life of its own.

Square Shooter Product Identity

This seemed a logical way to go when I could create a lot more tension with large black panels and much less type to position. The guys in Sales were almost apoplectic about the final box design. They wanted to write all over it, but Calderwood went with my suggestion that *Less is indeed More*.

We could stack product at point of purchase to make a dramatic presence among competitive product packages on which sales departments had plastered photos, copy and bullets.

1971. When I look around at most packaging today at point-of-purchase, I feel as if I were blessed to be able to get away with such a clean solution. The one exception seems to be design coming from Apple. They are a perfect example of how impact can be gained with restraint.

This version works best because it's perfect for stacking and creating seductive space for the consumer eye amidst the chaos of package design in the average high-volume retail outlet.

Oh, yes. 1971 was a good year—for all of us.

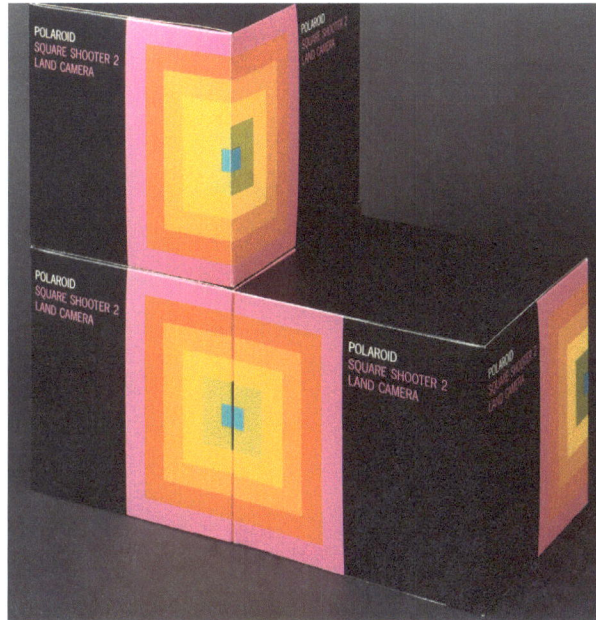

Despite the howls of protests from the sales guys who, as I said, wanted to write all over the packages—words like New! and all the stuff that everyone else says— they finally came around to liking what they saw at point-of-purchase.

Even the dimmest bulb in the photo department of a discount outlet could see that stacking these boxes in almost any way would draw floor traffic to Polaroid products.

Introduction of the Polaroid SX-70, 1972

This is a photo of the entire line at the time. The film box is at the bottom of the photo, surrounded by hardware boxes, which include an SX-70 Model 2, and a host of accessory items.

The word came down from on high that Land insisted on a white box, so we did a white box. For those (and there were more than a few) who complained of the simple solution, I countered that only *Chanel* managed to keep packaging this clean and identifiable over a whole range of products. For those others who would argue that Polaroid might possibly have too many images, would it have been better to use existing graphics and set in large type:

New!

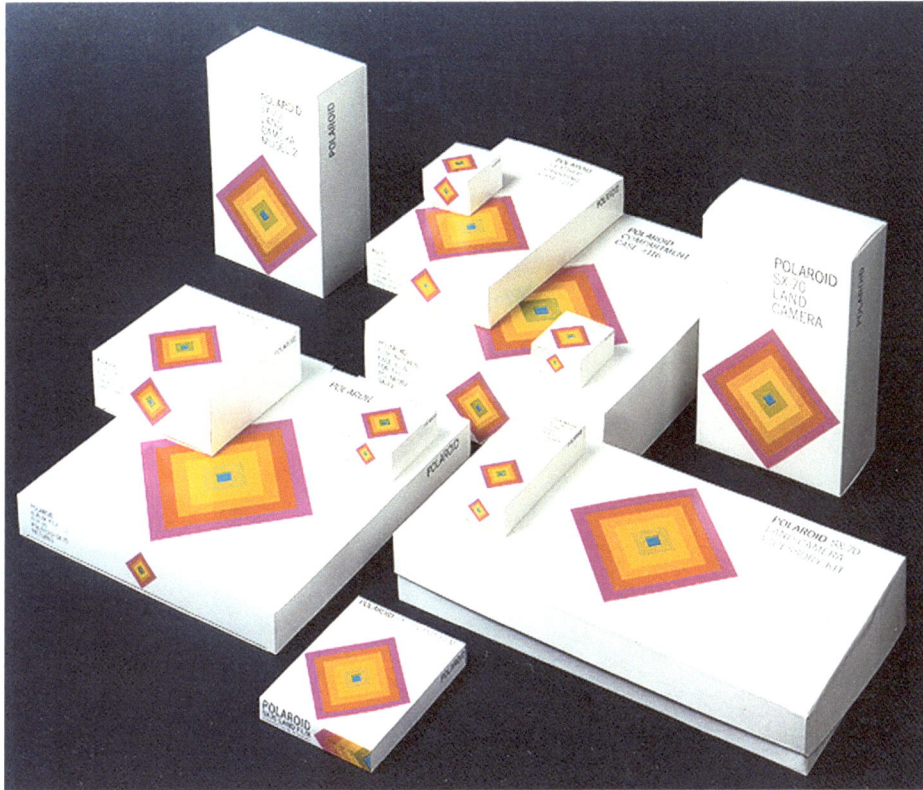

The gang's all here. Camera, film and accessory packaging resplendent in distinctive product image for the1972 introduction.

A year later, in 1973, I was assigned to design the graphics for an accessory kit for the SX-70 that included a panel to identify the individual accessories and how they might be used.

Polaroid's in-house packaging people did the structural design for the box, working with Champion, their folding box vendor.

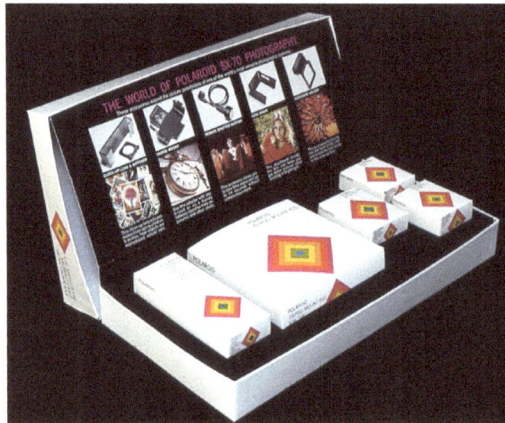

The SX-70 film process owes its existence to Lady Bird Johnson, First Lady and wife of President Lyndon B. She was offended by trash in our National Parks created by expended tabs of peel-apart Polaroid film and requested that Polaroid Corporation invent a neater picture process. They did—and the rest, as they say, is history.

POLAROID ALBUM #117

ALBUM #

POLAROID
SX-70
TELE/
1.5 LENS
#119A

POLAROID
CLOSE UP
LENS
AND
FLASH
DIFFUSER
#122

ALPHA 1

POLAROID SX-70   LAND CAMERA

POLAROID
LEATHER
CARRYING
CASE
(VINYL)

ODEL 3   EBONY

AROID SX-70   LAND CAMERA

POLAROID
LEATHER
CARRYING CASE
#28 FOR THE
POLAROID SX-70
LAND CAMERA

POLAROID
TRIPOD MOUNT #111
FOR THE
POLAROID SX-70
LAND CAMERA

POLAROID
LENS SHADE
#121

By 1975, the SX-70 family had grown considerably, and I had to come up with design variations without compromising the original product identity look.

Within a few years of its introduction, Polaroid SX-70 film ranked Number One in dollar sales in drugstores, creating more cash flow than Kodak Instant Film or Kodacolor II film, which followed in order as numbers two and three. In unit sales it was number eight compared to number six for Kodacolor II, but significantly ahead of Kodak Instant Film which is not shown on the chart (it was number fourteen). The article is from and copyright by The New York Times of August 1,1980.

Kodak instant color film "borrowed" my Polaroid color stripes as part of their graphics to identify their new product.

A New Picture at Drugstores

By BARBARA ETTORRE

Something new has entered the profit picture at the corner drugstore. These days the best-selling items are not aspirin, toothpaste, cold tablets or all the sundries one might expect.

The biggest-selling item is photographic film. More particularly, instant photographic film. That at least is the most prominent finding in a survey of the 100 top-selling items ranked by dollar volume by Drug Store News, a trade magazine. Of thousands of drug store products, Polaroid SX 70 film is No. 1 in sales, followed by Kodak Instant Film PR10 and Kodak Kodacolor II Film C110.

This comes as no surprise to the nation's leading drugstore chains, which for at least a decade have been increasingly stressing their sales of film and their film-developing business. In fact, they say, over the last three years, since the introduction of the Polaroid One-Step camera, instant film has supplanted regular film as their hottest seller.

"One of the major reasons for all this is the convenience of drugstores," said David Eisenberg, corporate vice president of marketing at Peoples Drug Stores, a $440 million chain with 500 stores in 13 states.

"We regard instant film as a highly 'consumerable' item — one that is consumed at one time," he said. "Generally, a person uses up one roll of 10 pictures and comes back for more."

Accordingly, drugstore retailers usually offer instant film, which sells at an average of $5.50 to $6 a roll, at very low markups, close to cost in some cases.

"We sell it at less than a 20 percent markup and near 5 percent or cost when it is on sale," Mr. Eisenberg said. "Our position is that we offer some kind of photo-related item — film, flash bulbs, and so forth — every week in our ads. Camera and film products produce about 5 percent of our total volume."

The Largest-Selling Drug Store Items

Ranked by Dollar Sales	Ranked by Unit Sales
1. Polaroid SX 70 Film	1. Crest Toothpaste (7oz.)
2. Kodak Instant Film PR10	2. Kodacolor II Film C110 (20 exp.)
3. Kodacolor II Film C110 (20 exp.)	3. Tylenol (100's)
4. Oil of Olay (4 oz.)	4. Colgate Dental Cream (9 oz.)
5. Tylenol (100's)	5. Tampax (40's)
6. Crest Toothpaste (7 oz.)	6. Kodacolor II C126 (20 exp.)
7. G.E. Flip Flash	7. G.E. Flip Flash
8. Polaroid Polacolor II Film	8. Polaroid SX 70 Film
9. Kodacolor II C126 (20 exp.)	9. Chapstick Lip Balm
10. Kodacolor II 135 (24 exp.)	10. Listerine (32 oz.)
11. Sylvania Flip Flash	11. Oil of Olay (4 oz.)
12. Tampax (40's)	12. Playtex Tampons (16's)
13. Colgate Dental Cream (9 oz.)	13. Bayer Aspirin (100's)
14. Listerine (32 oz.)	14. Kodak Instant Film PR10
15. Revlon Flex Hair Cond. (16 oz.)	15. Sylvania Flip Flash
16. Contac (10's)	16. Anacin (100's)
17. Playtex Tampons (16's)	17. Sylvania Magicubes (3-pack)
18. Pampers (12's)	18. Revlon Flex Hair Cond. (16 oz.)
19. Bayer Aspirin (100's)	19. Ban Roll On Deodorant (1.5 oz.)
20. Sylvania Magicubes (3-pack)	20. Bix Butane Disposable Lighter
21. Ban Roll On Deodorant (1.5 oz.)	21. Kodacolor II 135 (24 exp.)
22. G.E. Magicubes (3-pack)	22. Pampers (12's)
23. Revlon Flex Shampoo (16 oz.)	23. Contac (10's)
24. Nyquil (6 oz.)	24. Cricket Disposable Lighter
25. Stay Free Maxi Pads (30's)	25. Rolaids

Source: Drug Store News magazine

This is fine if the shopper buys instant film, since the need generates consumer traffic. But if a customer wants film requiring developing or photo-finishing, drugstore operators are very happy. This is where they make their profit in the film category — often a markup of more than 35 percent on the service.

They call this "the triple threat." A customer comes into the store three

Continued on Page 29

101

Polaroid Square Shooter Plus Product Identity

This was another curve thrown at us. First there were the Polaroid Colorpack cameras that used rectangular format film. Then, in an economy move, the Polaroid Square Shooters, which used less expensive (and smaller) square format film. Now, we were told, the engineers had come up with a camera that used BOTH film formats.

A great concept, but what will work to create product identity?

This is my solution. I think it solved the problem and created a very striking image, especially since product could be stacked in any number of configurations.

This product came after the Polaroid SX-70 (1972). I place it here to continue with the evolution of the color stripes and god's-eye product identity.

More stackable packages to create in-store traffic.

Sometime in 1976, the in-house package development guys came up with some new concepts for boxes that had been developed after recent crash-tests. So it was back to the drawing board, the typesetter, darkroom, light table and Cromalin to create designs such as the one shown on the opposite page.

The design plot thickened as product engineers cranked out more and more camera models to hit all the price points in the photographic market. Someone decided that the face plate of the camera should carry Polaroid color stripes because the ad brass decided to do their own corporate design in-house and that color stripes would be part of the identity program. I was not invited to contribute to this very significant overhaul. Since the product used the same film as SX-70, I kept that mark on the box. Then I found out that Sales didn't want it (for whatever reason) and I came up with this version.

It got shot down, too.

1976. Scanned from a 35mm Kodachrome slide, these are dummy boxes created with cut Letraset adhesive color film for the god's-eyes and 3-M Color Key type patches.

This is my final and accepted prototype.

You can see sell copy beginning to appear on the top of the box. It was becoming obvious that my influence had waned and there was no Stan Calderwood to call off the in-house attack dogs.

(Just by itself, the political intrigue at Polaroid in 1977 would take pages to describe and we won't go there because of space limitations.)

Polaroid OneStep Land Camera, 1977.

And Now for Something Completely Different

Type 105 Positive/Negative was a fun job to do, mostly because nobody cared about it even if it was to be one of Polaroid's best professional film products. I thought it would be great to go pos-neg with both graphics and type.

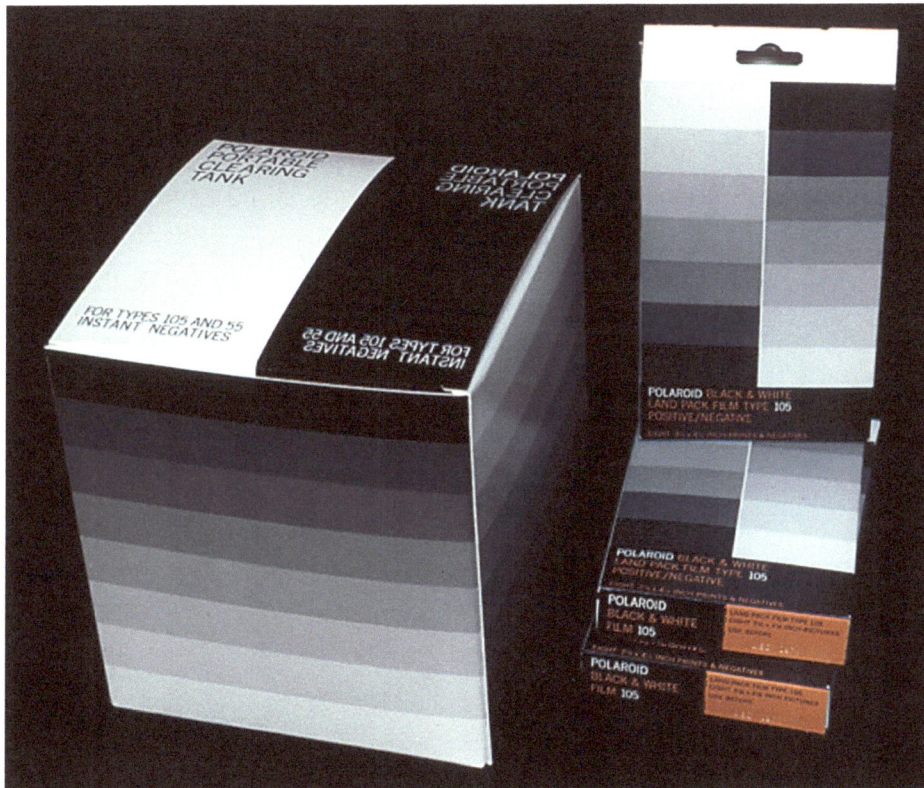

Designed and in production around 1973, the Polaroid Portable Clearing Tank and film box. *The tank contained Polaroid's version of acid fixer where the exposed negative was hung and then washed in water. The negatives weren't bad, but not much of a threat to conventional film sold by* Kodak, Ilford, or Agfa.

The Last Hurrah: Polavision

If there's one thing I can remember about those difficult days it's Stan Calderwood's opposition to a product that contributed, I feel certain, to his leaving the company. "Jee-zus, Gee-am," he would say in his (Chugwater) Wyoming twang,

"The goddam movie camera business accounts for only three per cent of the entire photographic market and Land insists on getting into it."

Polaroid Polavision product line, 1977. I used an enlarged image of traditional movie film with characteristic sprocket holes as the design device used on top of the traditional Polaroid color stripes.

I tested the product but it was obviously a turkey compared to anything I was using that Kodak offered, and a positive disaster when compared to my new Super 8mm Bolex. We leaned on design to make it look like a winner. The tinted plasic gave it an unwarranted classy look. Instant movie film was an engineering achievement, but it's precisely what separated Polaroid techies from Polaroid pragmatists.

There just weren't enough customers out there on whom to work the magic. Stan Calderwood's prediction of a financial disaster came in 1974 when Polaroid stock had plummeted to a fraction over 14 and stockholders lost considerably over $4 billion*.

This blow came even as SX-70 sales went through the roof and total sales approached $1 billion in 1976.

Land's personal losses were estimated at $660 million, according to Peter Wensberg in his book, *Land's Polaroid*.

----

*It's discouraging to consider what that money would have done for employees and the city of Cambridge if put to good use and not allowed to simply evaporate in the stock market.

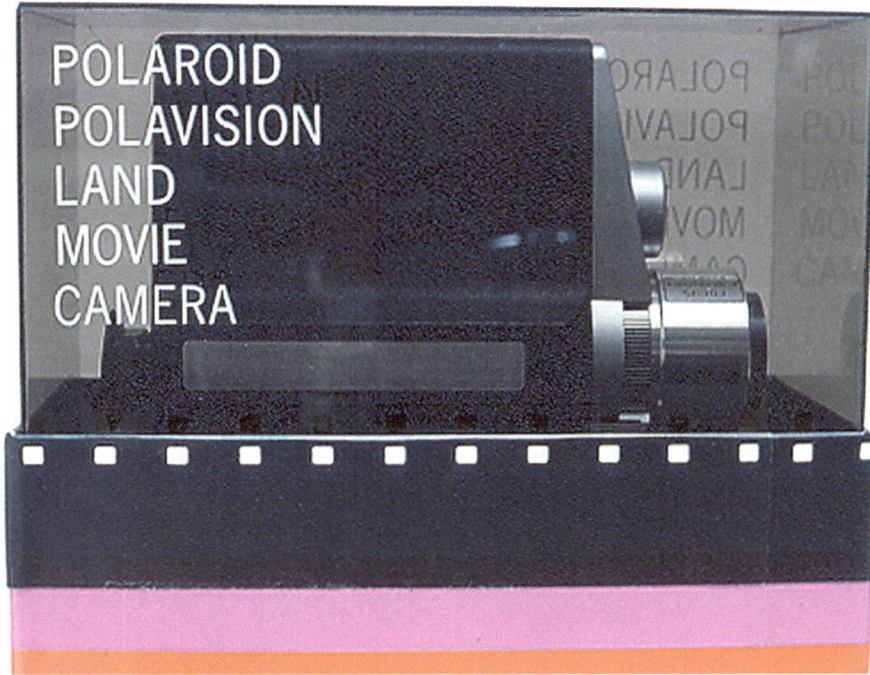

POLAROID
POLAVISION
LAND
MOVIE
CAMERA

The product was given a classy treatment with clear smoky plastic.

Polaroid Sunglasses (International)
As a Flag for Product Identity

This design was so strong as product identity that it became almost generic as a flag or symbol for sunglasses throughout Europe and elsewhere in the world, except for the USA and Canada where Polaroid had licensing deals with *RayBan, Foster Grant*, and other manufacturers to sell its sunglass products.

My favorite product identity. Polaroid Sunglasses International, 1962.
The blue and green bands and black sun became generic throughout
Europe to identify sunglass products.

The Polaroid sunglasses image of 1962 illustrate how the ubiquitous Polaroid color stripes evolved that were used to introduce Polaroid color film. These are the color stripes you see in previous pages and in the Iconongraphy graphic. This is a favorite assignment because I have always thought it to be one of my best solutions for a product identity flag. It's also one of the simplest and, as any designer will tell you, simple is the most difficult to do. This is the prototype for a counter card. The type was eventually changed to *News Gothic* [Regular] from its bold version seen here.

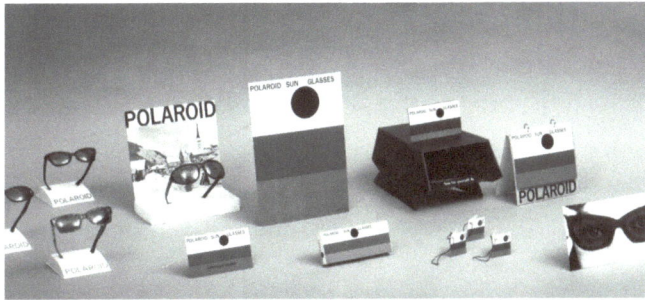

Variations on the theme. Compare the heavy use of Polaroid in bold with my solution on page 127 and directly below.

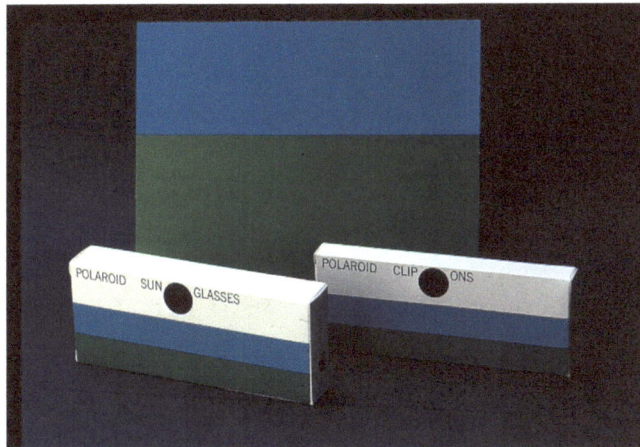

Polaroid sunglasses and clip-on packages for the international market. In the background is the large counter card seen above.

Is Graphic Design Art or Industrial Waste?

I don't know if graphic design is art, but I do know that it can be simply one more form of industrial waste. Like any reasonable person, I'm against further pollution of our environment. With all the lip service paid to originality and doing one's own thing, it is hard to explain the periodic avalanches of manneristic and trendy material that may initially have had some charm, but which is soon lost in indistinguishable and pervasive sameness.

The worst pollutants are the mindless displays of material that do not even approach this "me, too" level. They bring visual discomfort to our everyday lives and we must endure them along with the noise and foul air.

One has only to try to fill a shopping list in a supermarket or attempt to get from one part of a major U.S. city to another to experience the chaos that is contemporary packaging, promotional material, and signage.

From my essay in IDEA *magazine, Tokyo, 1972.*

My Studio/Workshop

I built my Cape Cod workshop/studio in 1962 with a carpenter and a stone mason. I worked as their helper until the building was ready for me to paint. It was a typical two-car garage in size, 20 x 24 feet, with an added ell of 8 x 12 feet, which housed a DuPont Cromalin machine and a UV-light burner for 3-M Color Keys. It was heated by two wall heaters that burned propane gas and was cooled in summer by a window unit air conditioner. I insulated the slab floor with tongue-and-groove pine flooring nailed to 2x10-inch boards set on end with fiberglass insulation in between.

A Velux skylight provided just the right amount of clear north light directly above my stand-up drawing table. It was a great work space that I used almost daily for twenty years.

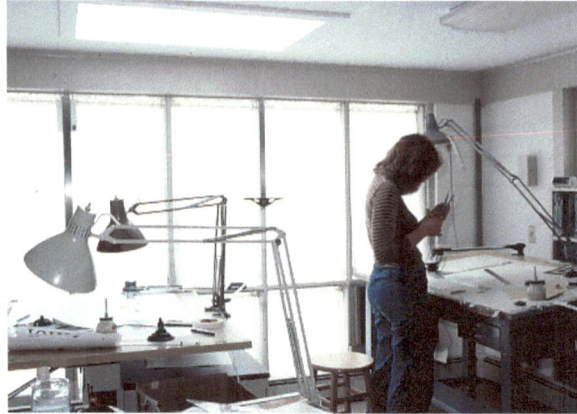

Two stand-up drawing tables are side by side directly in front of large long shelving. Opaque plastic panels provided a minimum of insulation but very good lighting from large windows.

An assistant pastes up a mechanical on a Hamilton drawing table using a drafting machine to line up reproduction type proofs she has cut apart.

A 10x12-foot darkroom was situated just behind the long shelves. On the left is an Agfa vertical camera, eventually replaced with a Danish Mullen electric eye model.

In the center is a Berthold Staromat machine for large display type. (These had output similar to that produced by Typositor machines made in the U.S.A.)

On the right is a dryer connected to a four-bath film processor, both made by Agfa.

All these items were necessary for what was referred to in the 1970s and 1980s as wet chemistry. They became almost totally worthless as digital technology eventually prevailed.

The Berthold Diatype required constant maintenance and occasional repair. There was no wysiwyg in those days—all typesetting was blind with reliance on German-English dictionaries.

Running a color proof from a DuPont Cromalin machine. To its left is a machine to burn 3-M Color Keys. A sheet of plate glass on which chemicals are applied sits on top of bumpers.

Unlike "wet chemistry" 3-M Color Keys, DuPont Cromalins were made by pouncing or rubbing powdered color on slightly tacky impressions made by exposing very thin film attached to light cardboard. Here I was using Kromekote supplied by Champion Papers.

I usually wore a simple dust mask because the color powder filled the air as I dragged a soft cloth over it to create the look of a printed impression. I have no idea if the powder was toxic because in those days there were no warning labels on such stuff, and OSHA had yet to be born.

That is a very shiny sheet metal tray with an attached vacuum that was fairly ineffectual. The trays held color-saturated rags that were in use.

Design Influences

Andrew Giambarba

I was fortunate enough to work and travel around Europe from Ireland to Italy via Scandinavia for seven months in 1955, the golden years of graphic and industrial design, influenced by Roman letters, above, and the contemporary designs of the modern Swiss, seen in this illuminated post office sign.

This example of Roman lettering incised in stone from the time of Jesus was as thrilling to discover as the wall paintings in the caves of Lascaux. Both are overwhelming evidence of man's incredible ability to dazzle us with extraordinary sophistication and technical ability.

In the immediate post-World War II period in Europe, it seemed that there was inspiration everywhere I looked.

Only the Swiss could take a prosaic battery of postal machines and turn it into an outstanding work of municipal design. This is from a 35mm. slide taken in Morges, a small city on the north shore of Lac Léman between Geneva and Lausanne. In 1959, my young wife and I lived in the maid's quarters of a villa in Prévérenges, a nearby village. Down the lake in Morges, film stars Audrey Hepburn and William Holden were in residence.

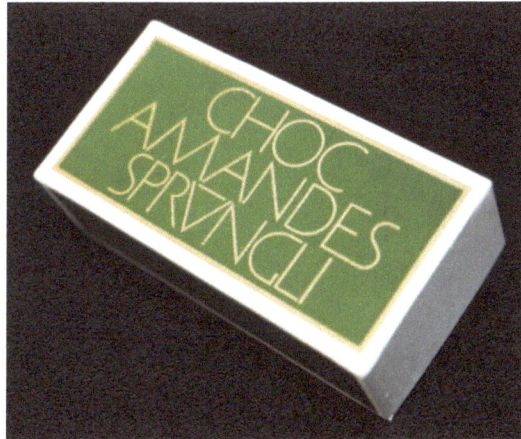

Two examples of extraordinary product identity using package design to establish a feeling of sophistication and classic good taste. Above, chocolate almonds from Lindt and Sprüngli, Zürich, in a simple box with a green panel and gold letters. Below, bath soap from Sweden in vivid colors.

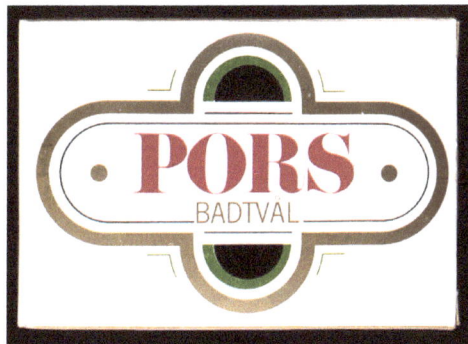

I chose not to be a Polaroid employee because I had already enjoyed the freedom of freelance life for ten years before I met up with Stan Calderwood. He delighted in chiding me with, "Gee-yam, you're just not made for corporate life!" He was right. I did a lot of travelling that wasn't business travel, and it was an education I would recommend to any young designer. In the years 1960 through 1963, I built myself a home and a studio on Cape Cod, fishing and swimming whenever my workload and weather permitted. I had the great experience of being with my wife and watching my children grow without the lost hours of commuting and working elsewhere. After expat adventures abroad and nine years of publishing Arts&Flowers greeting cards in Sonoma County, California, I returned to Cape Cod where I court the same muse of these Branding of Polaroid years.

Right: My poster for a regatta commissioned by the Yacht Club Costa Smeralda in 1972. I took a six-month contract to work for H.H. Aga Khan IV's hotels and consortiums on Sardinia while Polaroid was totally consumed in developing SX-70.

Epilogue
Stan Calderwood (1921-2003)
An Unabashed Tribute

This is how I want to remember Stan. The year was 1973, and Stan had been three years away from Polaroid and his boss, Edwin H. Land. We were at my favorite Boston restaurant, *Café Budapest*. (Yes, I know the photo is out of focus but so probably was I.) Upon leaving Polaroid, Stan took over as president of WGBH-TV public television in Boston. Within months he had swung a deal with the BBC to import *Masterpiece Theatre*, and then convinced Mobil Oil to fund it. Earlier, he arranged for Julia Child to introduce her series, *The French Chef,* to American television audiences. With this kind of phenomenal success, we were all sure that it wouldn't be long before Stan Calderwood would be running the entire Public Broadcasting network. Little did any of us know that before summer's end in 1970, he would be embroiled in a no-win situation with activists in Boston's black community. It was about the use of socially unacceptable profanity on prime time television. The irony here is that PBS lost a good man who had done what he could to help recruit minorities at Polaroid. Along with being insulted and jostled at confrontations, he began receiving death threats for cancelling Say Brother. Responding to public pressure, WGBH reinstated the show as Basic Black, calling the prior cancellation a "mistake." Stan quit. In 1972, he joined a money-management business controlled by Yale University and found his comfort level among kindred spirits in corporate management and the shepherding of institutional pension funds.

In 1981 he had accumulated enough personal wealth to buy control of Trinity Investment Management of Boston. By this time we rarely saw each other, let alone socialized with our wives as we once had, so I have no first-hand knowledge of him or Norma Jean in the last two decades of his life. I choose to remember Stan, the cowboy from Chugwater, Wyoming, via Scottsbluff, Nebraska, and Boulder, Colorado.

I'm sure he would prefer to be remembered as a Harvard Fellow and brahmin benefactor who, with Norma Jean, has endowed more university chairs and museums than many of his philanthropic contemporaries. Finally, it's my prejudiced opinion that if Edwin Land had not insisted that his successor be a fellow engineer and had encouraged and groomed Stan to run the company upon Land's retirement, Polaroid would never have lost its place as a leader in the world market nor would it have disenfranchised its retirees.

Stan departed this life at 81 on 10 May 2003 at Massachusetts General Hospital, where, typically, he was a significant benefactor.

Rest in peace *Big Spender from Chugwater.*

Rescued From Oblivion

With Dr. Florian Kaps, co-founder of The Impossible Project, Gmbh
at the introduction of the Paul Giambarba Polaroid Special Edition.
International Center of Photography, *New York, 18 December 2009.*

Doc Kaps traveled to Cape Cod in August of 2009 to have lunch and ask me to help him with his start-up venture, The Impossible Project. *I agreed and we proceeded to work together by email. The package designs above are part of the product identity I developed for the line of cameras and film called the* Paul Giambarba Edition. *Use of my name was Doc's idea, not mine.*

Integral film for Polaroid SX-70 cameras.

Doc and his business partners had bought up Polaroid film and cameras, then warehoused the lot in Europe. My packages are actually sleeves that slipped over packs of integral Polaroid film for SX-70 cameras above, and peel-apart Polaroid film for other Polaroid camera models.

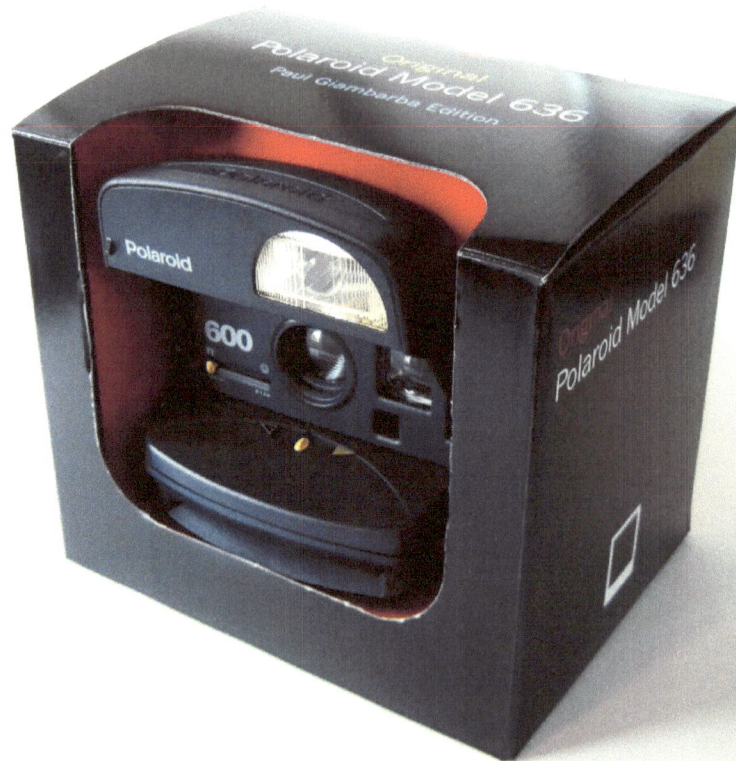

Polaroid Model 636 Paul Giambarba Edition *for* Impossible Gmbh,
*one of 20 package designs done in 20 days once I had final copy,
thanks to the advantages of working in this digital age.*

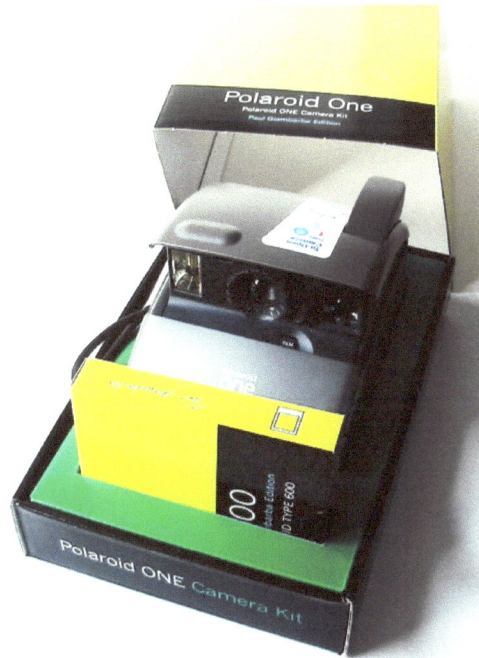

Camera kit and film Paul Giambarba Edition *for* Impossible Gmbh.

"The Impossible's new iteration, the Polaroid 600 One Kit comes in beautiful packaging designed by the guy who originally dreamed up Polaroid's iconic packaging, Paul Giambarba.

"Paul also designed the boxes for the group's film. Is it crazy that we also want to display these, along with the Polaroid 600 in our house? . . . ."
  —Sonia Zjawinski, *The New Polaroid as Decor, Apartment.*

Iconography of my Polaroid Product Identity, 1958-1977

1958 Polaroid all-purpose

1958 Polaroid photo products

1958 Polaroid corporate

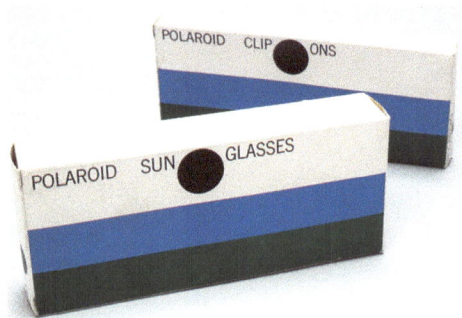

1962 Polaroid sunglasses

1968 Polaroid Colorpacks

1968 Polaroid Polacolor film

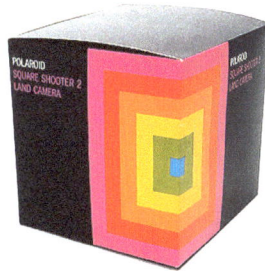

1970 Polaroid Square Shooters

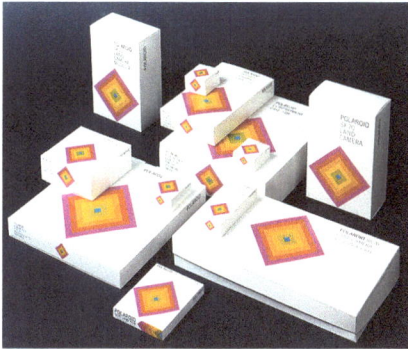

1972 Polaroid SX-70

1976 Polaroid Pronto! and One-Step

1977 Polaroid Polavision

The Ubiquitous Color Stripes

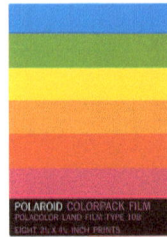

Giambarba Product Identity for Polaroid Colorpack products, 1968.

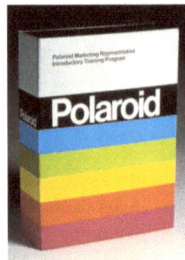

Polaroid Corporation, circa 1980.

Attributed to Rob Janoff, circa 1976, for Apple Corporation.

Prof. Achim Heine for Impossible Gmbh, 2010.

Some of the derivatives of my design device from the date of its first use for Polaroid packaging in 1968.

Advice to a Young Designer

Enjoy the moment. Things usually get worse.

Grant Hamilton

They say if you wait long enough—and I would add to that, live long enough—perhaps you might get the recognition you deserve. Certainly it has happened to me since I first uploaded *The Branding of Polaroid* web log in 2004. The quotes from John Weich's article in the U.K. publication, *Grafik*, for August of 2005 are more than I have ever expected to read about my work, and they are all the sweeter for having waited 25 years to know that the designs are appreciated in this graphic design world of following generations. I have had two articles published in Japan and one in the U.K. but nothing in the U.S.A. except for a brief appearance on television when CBS ran a segment on the apparent demise of Polaroid.

At the time of this 20-year window of Polaroid graphics, there were some prestigious awards given me by the Art Directors Clubs of Boston and New York in the form of Gold Medal awards and those of baser metals, as well as *AIGA Certificates of Excellence* from the American Institute of Graphic Arts in three successive package design shows for 1972, 1974, and 1976 and Walter Herdeg's influential *Graphis* magazine and his *Graphis Annuals* published some examples from time to time.

Though Polaroid paid all the entrance and hanging fees for my designs that were selected, I wasn't invited to the events. That was the way the class system at Polaroid functioned at the time.

The Nicest Compliment a Designer Can Get

Dear Sir,

    As I purchased two cartridges of Polaroid Colorpack film only because I so admired the attractive boxes in which they come, I am returning to you the two unused cartridges.

    Thank you for adding a little color to my life

              Sincerely,

Mt. Vernon, NY
       .10550

called

phone

does not own PL camera – really just liked boxes

2 – T108 no prices (mail rewrapped only)
        Undated L20727/BC

"Thank you for adding a little color into my life."

About the Author

As a sixteen-year old copy boy for the old *Boston Post*
I hand-lettered the news of the Japanese surrender that
ended World War II, thereby scooping the *Boston Globe*,
the Post's arch rival, just across Washington Street, where
crowds gathered to read the latest news chalked on
large hanging blackboards. My reward was a job in the
art department, which later led to a job as a daily sports
cartoonist for the old *Boston Herald*.

I attended Massachusetts School (now College) of Art and
studied with a mentor, Harold Irving Smith, an illustrator
and portrait painter who himself had studied with Robert
Henri and George Luks before World War I.

I've spent more than 65 years in the discipline of getting
images and text in ink and color on paper, as author and
illustrator, cartoonist, editor and publisher. In that time I
was also Polaroid's first art director and retained by them
for 25 years during which time the work shown in this
book was created.

www.ingramcontent.com/pod-product-compliance
Lightning Source LLC
Chambersburg PA
CBHW060812270326
41929CB00002B/16